Jesus' parable
from Luke 15:11–32
for children

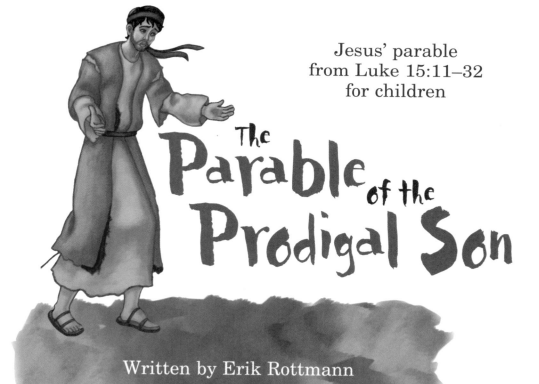

The Parable of the Prodigal Son

Written by Erik Rottmann

Illustrated by Shawna J.C. Tenney

CONCORDIA PUBLISHING HOUSE · SAINT LOUIS

Wherever our Lord Jesus went,
Large crowds would gather near.
The rich and poor and high and low
All pressed around to hear.

The tax collectors loved to come,
And other sinners too.
But Pharisees would shake their heads:
"This simply will not do!

"This fellow welcomes lowly folk!
He even shares their meals!"
So Jesus told a parable
Declaring how God feels:

There was a man who had two sons.
The younger said one day,
"I want my share of your estate,"
Then turned to go away.

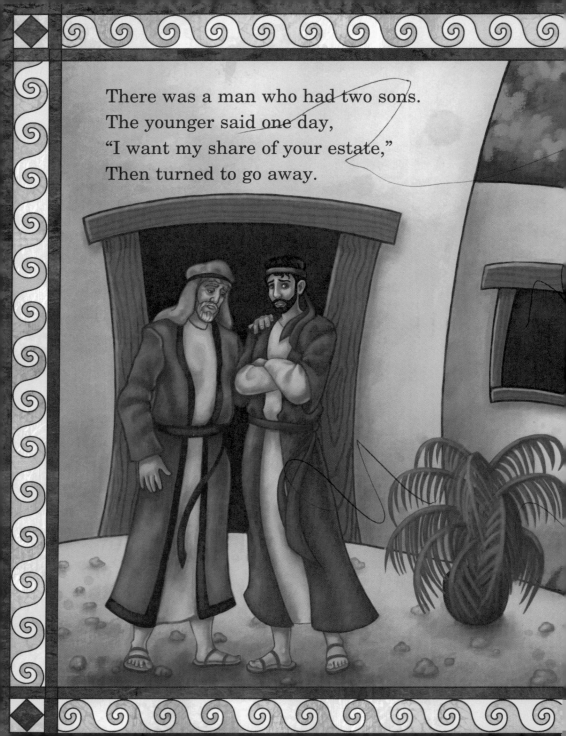

The father tried to stop his son.
The boy insisted, "No!"
So father sadly watched his child
Take everything and go.

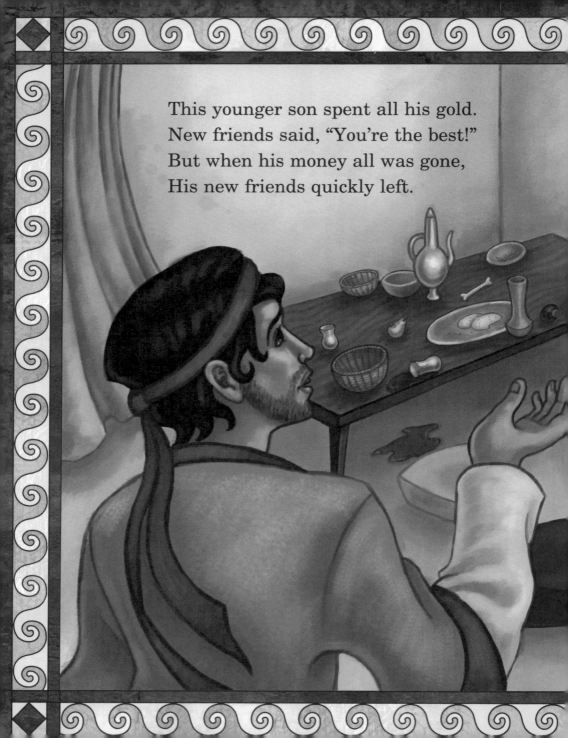

This younger son spent all his gold.
New friends said, "You're the best!"
But when his money all was gone,
His new friends quickly left.

So now the boy was all alone.
Then famine struck the land.
There was no money, food, or home.
There were no friends at hand.

Because the boy fell into need,
He found a lowly job:
A farmer sent him to the fields
To feed his hungry hogs.

The pigs ate pods—much better food
Than this boy had to eat.
His stomach felt so empty that
The pods seemed like a treat.

When he had suffered many days,
The boy said to himself,
"I must return to home again
To live like hired help.

"I am not worthy anymore
To bear my father's name
For I have squandered every gift,
And I accept the blame.

"I hope my father takes me back
To be his hired man.
If he will let me work for him,
I'll never leave again."

But while the boy was still afar,
His father saw him come.
He ran with joy to greet his child:
At last, the boy was home!

The father told his servants, "Go!
Bring him a golden ring!
Let's put the best robe on my boy!
Let's feast and dance and sing!"

Just as this father hugged his child
And brought the boy back in,
So God the Father welcomes you,
Forgiving all your sin.

When God made you His own in Christ,
He gave you His best robe:
He wrapped you in His Son, our Lord;
He cleansed and made you whole.

Dear Parents,

"His father saw him and felt compassion" (Luke 15:20). The Parable of the Prodigal Son (Luke 15:11–32) could also be called the Parable of the Forgiving Parent. A father patiently loves two sons: the younger, who sinfully ran away, and the older (not mentioned in this Arch Book), who sinfully resented both his younger brother and his father. Both sons needed repentance and forgiveness—and their father wholeheartedly forgave both of them! This parable provides you with a clear and simple way of teaching your children about the forgiveness our heavenly Father has for us on account of Christ's death and resurrection. Whenever we fall into sin, our Father in heaven welcomes us back in Christ!

This parable also illustrates how human parents will always love, forgive, and welcome their children, no matter what sins the children might commit. You could use this parable to discuss the suffering the younger son experienced because of his sin. Also focus your child's attention on the forgiveness the father gave, despite the son's rebellion. Such forgiveness does not give children permission to rebel! However, you can use this parable to assure your children that they are always loved and forgiven—by you and by our heavenly Father as well.

The Author